The Backstreet Boys

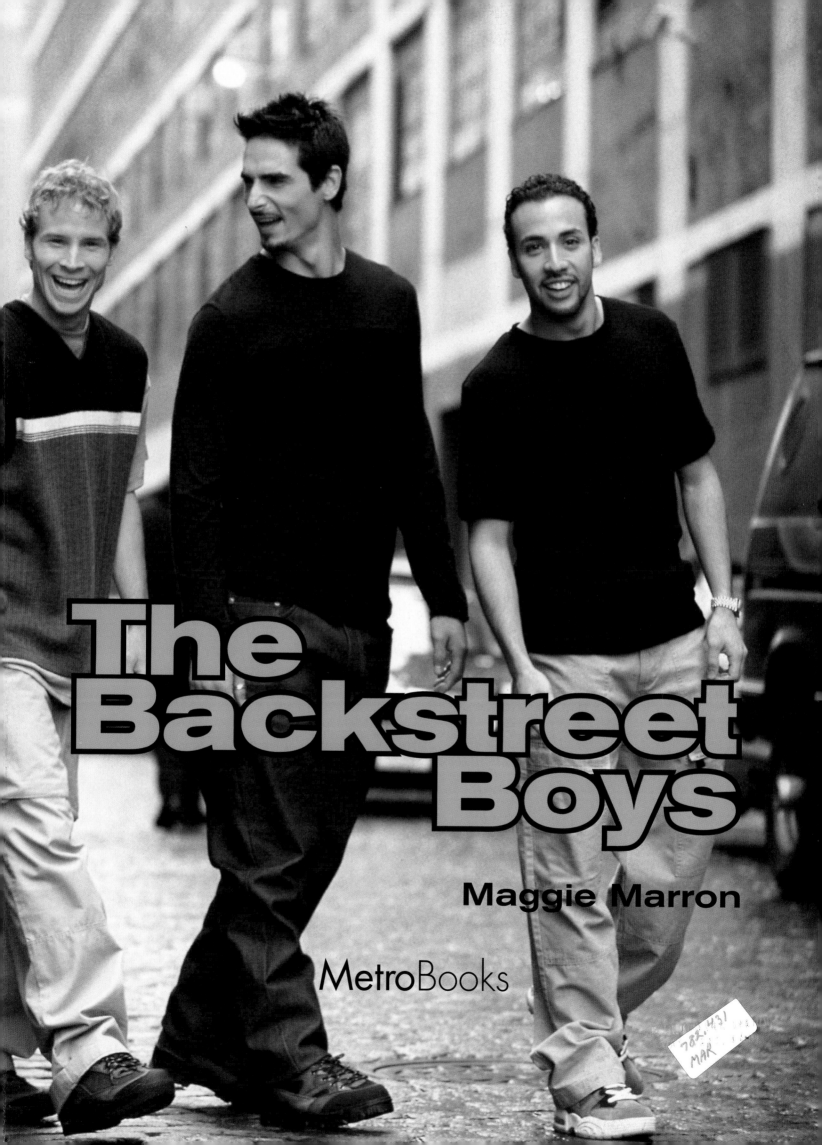

The Backstreet Boys

Maggie Marron

MetroBooks

Dedication
To Backstreet Bob M.

MetroBooks

An Imprint of Friedman/Fairfax Publishers

Library of Congress Cataloging-in-Publication
Data available upon request.

ISBN: 1-56799-947-6

Editor: Ann Kirby
Art Director: Kevin Ullrich
Designer: Liz Travato
Photography Editor: Valerie Kennedy
Production Director: Karen Matsu Greenberg

Color separations by Radstock Repro
Printed in England by Butler & Tanner Ltd.

3 5 7 9 10 8 6 4

For bulk purchases and special sales,
please contact::
Friedman/Fairfax Publishers
Attention: Sales Department
15 West 26th Street
New York, NY 10010
212/685-6610 FAX 212/685-1307

Visit our website:
www.metrobooks.com

The Boys, just before they
took off for Europe.
Clockwise from top: A.J.
McLean, Brian Littrell, Nick
Carter, Kevin Richardson,
and Howie Dorough.

12.99

Contents

Introduction

"We hope to be old people onstage together, as old as the Rolling Stones."

—Nick, in *USA Weekend,* January 1999

The guys look tough filming a commercial for Sears, the sponsor of their 1999 tour.

It seems like these days you can't turn on the radio or television or open a magazine without getting a glimpse of the Backstreet Boys—the five gorgeous hunks based in Orlando, Florida, who have captured the hearts of millions of women around the world with their excellent tunes and killer dance moves.

Sure, today the group might be a household name, but an overnight success the guys have not been—at least not in their native country. As a matter of fact, just a couple of years ago they could all be walking down a street in the States and no one would give them the time of day—let alone clamor for an autograph or a lock of hair. Now, all that's changed.

It took years of struggling—singing and dancing their hearts out, trotting across the globe, making records, getting signed, getting dropped, hiring managers, firing managers—and, for many of the guys, overcoming personal strife to get where they are today. And what if they had given up? Where would we be today without Nick's impish smile, or A.J.'s crazy tattoos, or Kevin's dreamy eyes, or Howie's impeccable sweetness, or Brian's velvety smooth voice? We'd be totally deprived of the experience of a lifetime—that's where we'd be!

The Backstreet Boys have made their way into our hearts for more than just their music. Each member is as interesting as the next and each is unique. And they're all very talented. "You usually don't get five people who can sing *a cappella* like they can, minus the engineers and producers," Hedy End, editorial director of *SuperTeen* and *Superstars* magazines, has said. Plus, these guys don't just sing; they dance, they write some of their own music, and most of them play musical instruments. And to top it all off—they're all cute!

The Backstreet Boys are everyone's favorite boys next door, and the guys who started it all—the ones who opened the door for acts like 'N Sync, 98°, and 5ive, and set a new standard in the contemporary music world. And the best thing about the guys is that they love their fans, probably even more than their fans love them! As they sing in their song "Larger Than Life" (a tribute to their fans): "All of your time spent keeps us alive . . ."

Now turn the page and learn the story of the sexiest guy group around!

Black leather jackets, black jeans, and black boots—
Backstreet Boys are stylin' on stage.

Chapter One
Beginnings

"Yeah, people will look at us and see an automatic stereotype. But once they hear us, they'll know we're for real."

—Howie, in *Entertainment Weekly,*
August 1997

The guys in London. The Backstreet Boys made a huge splash in London, while in their own country they were virtual unknowns.

There's more than one version out there of the story of how the Backstreet Boys got started. One story says that the group was the brainchild of talent manager Louis Pearlman, the "father" of such acts as 'N Sync. Another says that the guys were handpicked and assembled by the talent management firm The Wright Stuff. And yet another says that each of the guys was looking to fulfill the dream of becoming a world-class performer, and eventually they found each other. In a sense, all three stories are true.

Each member of the Backstreet Boys has a unique look, style, and talent, yet the quintet works incredibly well together. That's part of the group's appeal.

It was 1993 when Orlando-based management guru Lou Pearlman decided that the time was right once again to introduce a new guy group onto the music scene. There wasn't a group out there at that moment that tugged at the heartstrings and infiltrated the daydreams of young girls everywhere. By that time, the New Kids were "out"—way out. Instead, girls had to content themselves with messy grunge rockers like Nirvana's Kurt Cobain and Pearl Jam's Eddie Vedder. Pearlman brought in Johnny and Donna Wright, the masterminds behind the New Kids on the Block phenomenon, to get the project rolling. The Wrights quickly placed an ad in a national newspaper looking for talent to create a band in the vein of their last success story.

Nick and Brian mug for the cameras. All the Boys are as close as brothers.

What Makes the Backstreet Boys Stand Out?

The Backstreet Boys have certainly spawned their fair share of copycat acts, even one created by Lou Pearlman himself—we'll get to that in a minute! But what makes the Backstreet Boys a one-of-a-kind group? That's pretty easy to answer.

There are of course the obvious reasons. There's someone for everyone to love in the group. They're all different ages and each has his own look and distinct personality. And they can all sing—and how! On top of that, Howie and Brian both play the guitar, Nick is teaching himself the drums, and Kevin's been playing the piano by ear since he could walk—plus they all like to write their own songs.

At the heart of it, what really makes them strong is their dedication to each other. The Boys are like brothers, and it is this special bond that will keep them together for the long haul, while they develop their talents as a group. They've already been together for more than five years and have been through lots of struggles in that time and managed to stay together—what could possibly come between them now? As Nick told *Teen* magazine in September of 1998, "Several groups have let fans down by breaking up. We've been together for five years. We're gonna stick around." And A.J. continued, "Since the group started, it's always been five, and I don't think anybody's going anywhere fast. It will always be the five of us—[we're] like brothers."

"We're thankful we came first, but everybody that came behind us . . . we did a lot of opening doors [for them]," Brian confidently told *Teen People*. "I think we'll continue to do that." Of course Howie, Mr. Diplomacy, also acknowledged that "There were a lot of people who opened the doors for us before in the past. It's always just a process of helping each other out and stuff. Like I say, I don't look at it as a competition thing—if anything, it's a friendly competition."

Part of the supposed "rivalry" that the media likes to set up between 'N Sync and the Backstreet Boys is that they have the same "father," namely Lou Pearlman, though the Backstreet Boys came first. "That hurt our feelings," Kevin confided to *Rolling Stone*. "Because it was like, 'We're a family.' Then all of a sudden, 'It's business guys, sorry.' We have nothing against . . . that group personally. It was Pearlman not being honest."

The guys of 'N Sync have nothing against the Boys either. "Honestly," JC Chasez, the leader of the group told the *Los Angeles Times*, "they're busy doing their thing and we're busy doing ours."

Who has more staying power? Only time will tell, but it's nice to know that at the bottom of it all the guys in both groups might actually really be friends!

Backstreet Quiz How well do you know The Early Days

1) Before joining the Backstreet Boys, Kevin was working as:

a. Clown

b. Aladdin at Disney World

c. Waiter

d. Ice-cream man

2) Who was the last Boy to sign up?

a. Howie

b. Nick

c. Brian

d. A.J.

3) Which Boy has other famous family members?

a. Nick

b. Kevin

c. A.J.

d. Howie

4) Which guy's mother wrote a best-selling book about his early days?

a. A.J.

b. Howie

c. Nick

d. Kevin

5) Which Boy has always read the Bible to wind down from a crazy day?

a. Brian

b. Howie

c. Nick

d. A.J.

Answers: 1: b; 2:c; 3:a; 4: c; 5: a

In the meantime, the everyday, ordinary guys that would become the international superstars they are today were leading pretty everyday, ordinary lives. Florida natives Howie Dorough and A.J. McLean, who today are best buds, had gotten acquainted on the Florida talent circuit, often bumping into each other at the same auditions. The two of them began to pal around together at the auditions, until they started to notice another kid—a blond-haired, blue-eyed crooner who could sing like nobody's business. And then there were three.

Nick Carter, Howie, and A.J. became very serious about performing with each other and even got a group together and performed as an *a cappella* act. They called themselves "The Backstreet Boys" after a market in Orlando where kids hang out. One day, while shuffling through the entertainment-jobs section of the paper, they came across the Wrights' ad. Convinced that this was the right way for them to go, the guys answered the ad and promptly auditioned. They almost all didn't make it in, however—but not for lack of talent. Howie had changed his name for the audition to "Tony Donetti," and in the shuffle of all the guys who came through the door for the audition, his "name" was misplaced. It's a good thing his pals Nick and A.J. landed their spots. They were able to clear up the confusion; the slots were then more than half filled.

Elsewhere in Florida, Kentuckian Kevin Richardson was working as Aladdin in the Disney World theme park when he came across the same ad. Although he was enjoying his stint as the famous Disney character by day, and spinning discs and clubbing by night, he knew somehow that this sounded like what he had been looking for all along. Kevin auditioned and became the fourth Backstreet Boy. It was a nightmare, though, trying to fit in the last piece. "I saw two people, and it was pretty bad," Kevin told *Rolling Stone*. "It just made me sad. And I said, 'You know what? I have a cousin who can sing his butt off.'" Brian Littrell auditioned, and the Backstreet Boys as we know them today were born.

The next step was to get this baby group the attention it deserved—and, of course, a record label to sign them. There was no doubt about the group's talent. Donna Wright told the *Los Angeles Times*, "My whole career, I've always gone with instinct. When I first heard the Backstreet Boys, I got the chills so strong that the hairs stood up straight on the back of my neck. I could just tell there was something there." Now it was just a matter of convincing the rest of the world.

Opposite: An early shot of A.J.—pre-tattoos, wacky hair, and crazy get-ups.

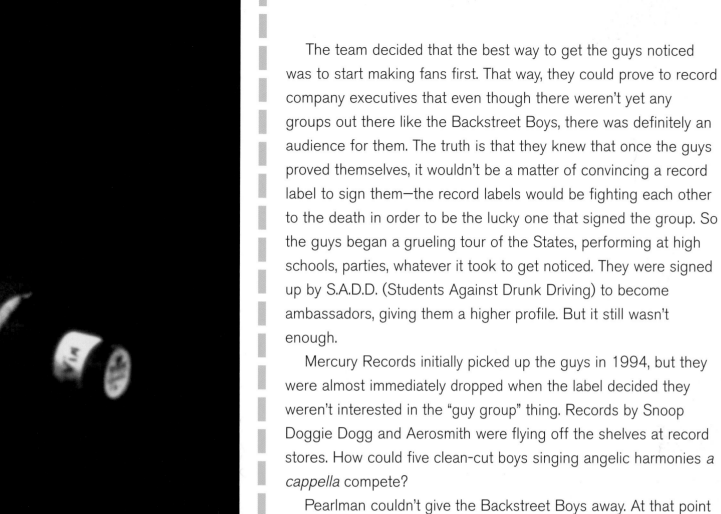

The team decided that the best way to get the guys noticed was to start making fans first. That way, they could prove to record company executives that even though there weren't yet any groups out there like the Backstreet Boys, there was definitely an audience for them. The truth is that they knew that once the guys proved themselves, it wouldn't be a matter of convincing a record label to sign them—the record labels would be fighting each other to the death in order to be the lucky one that signed the group. So the guys began a grueling tour of the States, performing at high schools, parties, whatever it took to get noticed. They were signed up by S.A.D.D. (Students Against Drunk Driving) to become ambassadors, giving them a higher profile. But it still wasn't enough.

Mercury Records initially picked up the guys in 1994, but they were almost immediately dropped when the label decided they weren't interested in the "guy group" thing. Records by Snoop Doggie Dogg and Aerosmith were flying off the shelves at record stores. How could five clean-cut boys singing angelic harmonies *a cappella* compete?

Pearlman couldn't give the Backstreet Boys away. At that point the labels had other plans. "It was hard. Lou shopped the group to ten different labels and nobody was interested. Everybody said the so-called boy band thing is over. Nobody knew these guys or wanted to," Alan Siegel, a longtime associate of Pearlman, told the *Los Angeles Times*. But Pearlman wouldn't give up. He fought to get the Boys a deal, and they were finally signed to Jive Records, a fairly new label under the Bertelsmann Music Group umbrella, in 1994. There was a lot of excitement when the Boys released their very first single, "We've Got It Goin' On," in October of 1995.

No one involved, from the guys to the Wrights to Lou Pearlman to the executives at Jive, thought they could lose. But they were wrong. The song peaked at an obscure number sixty-nine on the charts. The world at large still didn't know about the Backstreet Boys.

Kevin performs one of his solos in concert.

Above: Nick at the *Millennium* press conference—a tangerine dream!

Opposite: Nick belts out a solo during the 1997 U.S. tour.

Nickolas Gene Carter was born in Jamestown, New York, in the same hospital as the legendary comedienne Lucille Ball. Did that have anything to do with his eventual fame? Maybe a teeny tiny bit, but Nick is all talent, which his family acknowledged at a very early age (it had to have been early—Nick was only thirteen when he signed up with BSB!). When Nick was six, his parents moved the family—Nick and his baby sister BJ—to Tampa Bay, Florida.

Nick's first crack at show business was a leading role in a school production of *The Phantom of the Opera*. (No, he didn't play the phantom! He played the romantic lead, Raoul.) His performance got raves and prompted him to start a career in acting. At nine years old, he began doing commercials—both local and national—and then decided what he really loved more than anything was singing.

In the early 1990s, Nick auditioned for *The Mickey Mouse Club*, the same show that would launch the careers of Britney Spears, Keri Russell, and 'N Sync members Justin Timberlake and JC Chasez. But another opportunity was looming not too far off in the distance. By this point, Nick had already befriended Howie Dorough and A.J. McLean, and the three had formed a singing group together. When the offers to become a Mouseketeer or a Backstreet Boy came through at nearly the same time, Nick had a hard decision on his hands. *The Mickey Mouse Club* was already well established; the Backstreet Boys would be the riskier choice. But Nick decided to take that chance, which was the best career move he could have made—*The Mickey Mouse Club* was canceled shortly after Nick was offered a part.

Above: Nick poses with his mom, Jane, at a signing for her book, *The Heart and Soul of Nick Carter*.

Opposite: Nick showing off his dance moves onstage.

The World Famous Carter Brothers!

The Carter family sure has a lot to brag about these days! Not only is their oldest boy, Nick, a superstar with the Backstreet Boys, but Nick's brother, Aaron, has also caused a sensation in his own right. Just eleven years old, Aaron—whose favorite thing about being a pop star is that "fans give me candy all the time!"—has become a name well known and revered not only in his own country but all over Europe, in Asia, and in Canada as well.

So is there any rivalry between the two brothers? Not any more than there would be between any other pair of siblings. But the pair benefits from a lot of support and encouragement for each another. For example, Aaron was the opening act on the Backstreet Boys 1998 tour. Also, Nick, with the help of BSB "brother" Brian Littrell, wrote a couple of the songs on Aaron's album, *Surfin' USA*, including, "Ain't That Cute." As for Aaron's part, he's looking forward to his big brother making lots of appearances on his new TV show, which is in the negotiations stage at this writing.

Lucky Nick: Not many guys are fortunate to have so many great brothers!

Brian is known as "the shy one," and this could not be more true. It even comes out in his performance style. For instance, during the show he likes singing his solo while sitting in a chair, strumming his guitar. "It's a very personal experience and that's what I wanted it to be," he told *Teen Beat.* "Sitting down—if they didn't want to scream than they didn't have to, they could just sit and listen and watch. That was my whole idea because the show

Brian acts as ball boy for Arthur Ashe Tennis Day.

Brian relaxes during a photo shoot for Sears. The company is sponsoring the BSB '99 tour.

Backstreet Quiz How well do you know...**Brian?**

1) Brian's favorite movie is:
a. *You've Got Mail*
b. *Scream*
c. *Star Wars*
d. *The Breakfast Club*

2) What's Brian's favorite food?
a. Fried chicken
b. Macaroni and cheese
c. Steak
d. Tacos

3) Brian's favorite color is:
a. Midnight blue
b. Burnt orange
c. Forest green
d. Bright red

4) Brian is most afraid of:
a. Spiders
b. Heights
c. Snakes
d. Enclosed spaces

5) Brian's favorite movie
   actress is:
a. Julia Roberts
b. Elizabeth Hurley
c. Meg Ryan
d. Sandra Bullock

Answers: 1: c; 2: b; 3: a; 4: b; 5: d

is so bing, bang, boom, and then we have the five solos, and even those are bing, bang, boom, and I'm not really like that . . . when it can be really personal, I just walk out, show people who I am."

Brian certainly likes the attention of his fans but, like Nick, as well as the other guys, he wants to be appreciated for his talent, not just his sex appeal. Sometimes he doesn't even understand why girls get themselves so worked up when they see him. He told *Rolling Stone* that when they approach him, "[I] say, 'I'm human, it's no big deal.'"

Brian pals around with all the guys, but Nick Carter is definitely his best friend—despite their age difference and the way Nick has picked on his accent: "When I first met [Brian], I thought, COUNTRY BUMPKIN! It was crazy! 'Heyyy, howww ya'lll dooooin'? My name's Briaaaaan Littrell,'" Nick laughed, in *SuperTeen*. When Howie, Kevin, and A.J. hit the club scene, Brian stays in with Nick—who's under twenty-one—and the two play video games. They have become such great friends, in fact, that they are known in the band—and to their fans—as Frick and Frack.

The Boys on stage.
Touring is fun, but it's
also hard work.

Chapter Four

Around the World...in 730 Days

"[International] success
has made us more well
rounded. It changed our
perspectives on the way
the world is."

—Kevin, in *Billboard*
magazine,
November 1997

When the guys couldn't even hail a cab in the States in 1995, they headed across the pond to try their luck in foreign markets. What an experience it proved to be for them. Such excitement! Such hysteria! The world hadn't seen anything like it since the Beatles touched down on American soil more than thirty years earlier.

For the next two years, the Backstreet Boys would tour almost nonstop (how about five tours in one year!), which put a toll on their lives in more ways than one. Although the stardom was exhilarating, the guys really missed home.

All the Boys are very close to their families and no attention from their fans could replace the void they often felt on the road. "We like our families to be able to turn on the TV and see what we're doing," Kevin told *People Weekly*. Still, it wasn't the same as being home with them. They missed ". . . our families, our home-cooked meals, our own beds," Howie has admitted. A.J. agrees and is sad that fame "really limited our time with our friends and families," but added that "You can kind of get better Christmas presents for your family and stuff like that."

BACKSTREET QUIZ How well do you know . . . **The Backstreet Tour Experience?**

1) Which Boys love to dine in different countries, getting a sample of that country's cuisine?
a. Howie and A.J.
b. Nick and Brian
c. Kevin and A.J.
d. Kevin and Howie

2) Which of the Boys toured South America—without the others?
a. Howie
b. Kevin
c. A.J.
d. Nick

3) Where did "We've Got It Goin' On" first hit number one?
a. Sweden
b. Germany
c. France
d. Canada

4) Which Boy refuses to eat dairy products before a performance because he fears they cloud his voice?
a. Nick
b. A.J.
c. Brian
d. Kevin

5) Who takes the longest to get ready for a show?
a. Brian
b. Kevin
c. A.J.
d. Nick

Brian, A.J., Nick (sticking his tongue out), and Howie—is Kevin taking the picture?

Answers: 1: d; 2: a; 3: b; 4: d; 5: c

Being away from their families is not something the guys really want to get used to. And then there was Brian's heart problem . . .

The Boys got their first taste of superstardom in Germany, where their single "We've Got It Goin' On" reached number one almost as soon as it hit the airwaves. The Boys will all tell you that their experiences in Europe were a trip and a half! The fans were, well, fanatical, and they would show up in the oddest places just to get close to the guys. Brian remembered for *USA Today* that, one day, "I drove into my apartment complex, and they know my car because a picture of it had been in a magazine. And these two girls—one was from Germany and one was from Switzerland—were sitting right in front of my apartment with their pens and paper, and they jumped as soon as they saw me."

Howie agrees that their European fans were definitely aggressive. "We used to talk to fans in the hotel lobby, but we can't be as personable with our European fans because the hype is so big over there," he said in *Teen* magazine. Nick confirmed, in

Brian and Nick can find fast food anywhere! Here in Amsterdam they sample pommes frites—french fries—while relaxing before a show.

USA Today, that "We've been on radio stations in Germany and had to climb out of the windows to get out of the place. But in the end, it's all fun. We sit and laugh about it."

Meanwhile, while all this was going on, they were nobodies in their own country. "It was weird, because we'd play shows to, like, 10,000 fans in Europe, then we'd come back home and walk down the street and no one would recognize us," Nick told the *Los Angeles Times*. "It was a humbling experience, because now we want to show everybody 'Look, this is what we've been doing.'"

The world tour experience was very important, however, because it helped establish traditions the guys still practice today—especially the preshow prayer and hug. "It's like saying, 'Let's not take any of this for granted. We're blessed.'" A.J. said in *USA Weekend* in January 1999.

So have the Backstreet Boys kept up their momentum in Europe? You bet! *Backstreet Boys* sold millions of copies worldwide and it had gone gold or platinum in more than twenty countries— even though in their own country, in 1995 and 1996, no one except their families and friends had ever heard of the Backstreet Boys.

Howie croons for his fans—they're dying just to touch his hand!

Ever since Howie was three years old, singing "Baby Face" at the top of his lungs standing on his grandmother's bed, his older sister Polly Anna had been encouraging him to go into show business. In fact, Howie's first stage role was in a production of *The Wizard of Oz*, to which his sister had dragged him along for an audition. Polly Anna was cast as Glenda, the good witch; Howie made his stage debut as a munchkin!

Half Irish, half Puerto Rican, Howie was born in Orlando, Florida, the late-born last child of Hoke and Paula Dorough. Needless to say, with ten years between Howie and the second youngest, Johnny, Howie grew up the family's darling—but he was by no means spoiled. Howie's father retired from the police force when Howie was twelve and became Howie's main caregiver. Howie grew up with a sense of self-discipline that has served him very well throughout his career.

Howie had made the most significant career leaps at the time he met up with A.J. and Nick. In addition to singing in the church choir as a child and performing in all sorts of school productions, Howie had already been in two films: *Parenthood* and *A Cop and a Half*—not to mention countless Disney commercials. Like A.J., he also tried out for *The Mickey Mouse Club* and didn't make it. He also auditioned for Menudo at one point, but no dice. When he got together with A.J. and Nick, though, he knew they were on to something special.

Howie is a firm believer in the kind of music the Backstreet Boys make—despite the fact that his male peers don't always see the value in what they're doing. He remembered, in *Rolling Stone*, that during their first tour—before the single, even before they had signed a recording label—"The guys would heckle us. We'd say 'You think you can do better, come on up here.' We'd sing *a cappella* and we'd have them sing along with us. When it was their turn, we'd just drop out, let them sing by themselves. It embarrassed the heck out of them." This sounds so typical of Howie, who can

Above: Howie at the 1997 Billboard Music Awards.

Opposite: Howie struts his stuff at a celebrity basketball game in Miami in January 1999.

get through to anyone, no matter what situation the guys have ever found themselves in.

Howie can talk to anyone about anything at anytime—and make it make sense. In fact, he's often called in to settle fights between the guys and find some kind of peaceful resolution. And it usually works. He's the same way with his fans. Out of all the Boys, Howie always knows the right thing to say to any fan he meets. That's why his fans sometimes call him "Sweet D."

Out of all the guys, Howie is the most concentrated on the future. He wants to enjoy a long career with the Backstreet Boys—as well as a luxurious present!—but he's a show business veteran who knows all this could be over when he wakes up in

Howie and buddy A.J. in a brotherly embrace.

the morning. He's the proverbial squirrel preparing for winter. Howie has used his earnings to invest in condos, and, in addition to being a Backstreet Boy, he has gotten himself involved in real estate full time—which is why the guys all tease him and call him "the businessman." But he remains practical. "We've had some tough times," he told *Teen People*. "We want to thank the fans who've not believed the hype. It's made us stronger."

In addition to concentrating on his singing, Howie is starting to get more involved with the music, writing songs and playing instruments. "We just kind of dabble with [musical instruments]," he explains. "We're not trying to proclaim to be musicians, you know, professional musicians or anything. We're not trying to be the Hansons or anything." But he's serious about it. "I just got my home studio installed, and Nick just got his installed, too. So whenever we come home, now, all the ideas we have we can put them down and get them on tape and send them to the record company. And that's a lot of fun."

Nice hat, Howie!

BACKSTREET QUIZ How well do you know . . . Howie?

1) What was Howie's best subject in school?
a. History
b. English
c. Math
d. Biology

2) What's Howie's favorite kind of food?
a. Chinese
b. Cuban
c. French
d. German

3) Howie's favorite actor is:
a. Denzel Washington
b. Harrison Ford
c. Adam Sandler
d. Tom Hanks

4) Howie's favorite beverage is:
a. Coke
b. Sprite
c. Snapple
d. Milk

5) What was Howie's stage name for the BSB audition?
a. Mike Philips
b. Tony Donetti
c. Richard Smits
d. Jack Sprat

Answers: 1: c; 2: a; 3: d; 4: b; 5: b

Chapter Seven
American Invasion

"People think we're from London or someplace. But now it's time to come home. It's important for us to be recognized here."

–Brian, in *Entertainment Weekly*, August 1997

Backstreet Boys back-stage—all decked out at the Grammy Awards.

VIRGIN BOOKS

BSB versus NKOTB: Why BSB are here to stay

Part of the unfortunate backlash that the Backstreet Boys have received is that "they're just another New Kids on the Block," which is very upsetting for true Backstreet Boys fans because it just isn't so.

There are many reasons that they get burdened with this comparison, and they're all very aware of it. "We get that just because of our look and our age and everything," Nick told *USA Today.* "But comparing our style to theirs, we have a lot more R&B influences there."

Aside from their age, they also get knocked because they had the same management as the New Kids, namely Donna and Johnny Wright. But even the Wrights, as well as the big executives at the record compa- ny, know how special the Backstreet Boys are. "The difference is that these boys can really sing, and that's a major part of our marketing strategy," Jive Records VP of A&R David McPherson has said. "We're trying to get the media to look at them differently than the New Kids and present opportunities for them to sing in public, so people can see how talented they really are."

Kevin is usually responsible for keeping the group grounded, like a good older brother should be. The rest of the guys love him dearly, but they also respect his decisions and usually don't cross him. In the beginning, there was a little trouble between Nick and Kevin, because Kevin was so much older and Nick was such a practical joker—but all that's been resolved now. Kevin's taught Nick to be more serious; and Nick's taught Kevin to enjoy a good joke!

"I wish people would realize that we have the goods and that we're legit," Kevin told *Rolling Stone*. "We're talented, and we're not some flash in the pan. We've been together for six years." And if Kevin has anything to say about it, the guys will continue their success, earning the respect in the industry that they truly deserve.

Opposite: Kevin enjoys one of the perks of super-stardom as an honorary ball boy at Arthur Ashe Stadium.

Right: Kevin holds the roses given to him by adoring fans at a party held at the Hammerstein Ballroom before a New York concert.

Opposite: Kevin and Nick get chummy with Sean "Puffy" Combs.

Above: Gorgeous Kevin got to walk down the runway at the VH-1 Fashion Awards, where this luscious shot was snapped.

BACKSTREET QUIZ How well do you know . . . Kevin?

1) Kevin's favorite color is:
a. Sea green
b. Eggplant purple
c. Royal blue
d. Coral

2) If you made dinner for Kevin, he'd really like:
a. Tacos
b. Sushi
c. Burgers and fries
d. Spaghetti

3) Kevin's favorite actress is:
a. Sandra Bullock
b. Michelle Pfeiffer
c. Laura San Giacomo
d. Jennifer Love Hewitt

4) What's Kevin's favorite flick?
a. *The Spy Who Shagged Me*
b. *The Untouchables*
c. *Top Gun*
d. *Better off Dead*

5) For the first years of his life, Kevin and his family lived in a:
a. Trailer
b. Mansion
c. Log cabin
d. Apartment building

Answers: 1: c; 2: a; 3: b; 4: c; 5: c

Chapter Nine
Millennium . . .
and Beyond

"If we each had a song, written by each of us with our individual tastes, it would be the most outrageous album. Everything from rock, to gospel ballads, to hip-hop—it would be insane."

—A.J., in *Teen Beat*, August 1999

Showing off their various tastes in fashion, the Boys stop for paparazzi during their 1997 tour of London.

Backstreet Boys went ten times platinum and was nominated for a Grammy. How were the guys ever going to top that? "We had so much success with the first album, [it] set us apart from everyone else," Brian told *Teen People*. But would that success carry the second one? Well, record store owners around the country were convinced that the next album, *Millennium*, would not only top *Backstreet Boys* but would set some records of its own!

Around the country, record stores expected a landslide of buyers when *Millennium* became available on May 18, 1999. They even speculated that *Millennium* would break all records for sales on its release. They were right. *Millennium* sold about 500,000 copies on its first day out—and that's not all. It also broke the record for debut-week sales set by Garth Brooks the previous year.

So what's the secret of *Millennium*'s success? "The Backstreet Boys delivered a great album, with great songs, and have worked hard over the last several years to be in this position," was Jive Senior VP/GM of sales and marketing Tom Carrabba's answer to *Billboard* magazine.

That's not all. This time, members of the group really

made their voices heard by cowriting some of the songs. Brian cowrote "Larger Than Life," which he explains is a song about the way their fans make the guys feel. "The song is all about the fans," Brian explained to *Teen Beat*. "It talks about how they affect our lives and our reality . . . when you're onstage . . . you see all these people singing your songs. It makes you feel, larger than life." Brian also lent his writing talents to the ballad "The Perfect Fan," which, he explains, is "a song about my mom . . . everyone can relate to someone who pushes you in the right direction and is there to watch over you, and help you take those steps towards the good life."

"Back to Your Heart" was cowritten by Kevin, and if you ask him if it's personal, he might confess that he may have had a special lady in mind when he wrote it. Most of the other songs were written by Max Martin, most poignantly "Show Me the Meaning of Being Lonely," which the guys see as a tribute to Denniz Pop. Martin, the Swedish song spinner who has composed tunes for such huge acts as Britney Spears and Ace of Base, was convinced that this album was his best work yet. "I've never been

The guys indulge in an upbeat number during their most recent U.S. tour.

so happy with an album," he beamed in *Teen People*. "The last album was huge, so all the [new] songs had to be hits basically, and that's not easy," he continued. "The pressure is there; you just can't touch it. You can't really talk about it, because that will make them [more] nervous."

Things were not initially that smooth with the new album, however, especially when they proposed the name. Nick recalled that "we got a lot of flack from record company reps for naming it *Millennium* because they were like, 'Oh that's so corny.' We like the name. . . . I was actually afraid someone else would use [it]." Brian is totally confident that the right name was chosen. "Bring in the *Millennium*. Bring in the Backstreet Boys," he told *Teen People*. "How else would you want to bring it in but with a slamming record."

One of the best things that happened to the guys is that they picked up a great sponsor for the *Millennium* Tour: Sears. Look for the guys in print and TV ads for the famous store. Now the Backstreet Boys will be able to do the kind of show they've always dreamed of doing, a show worthy of their exquisite talents. Not that their other shows have been mediocre. Not even close. The performances are always an explosion of sound and light and energy and costume and dance. It will be absolutely exciting to see what the new show will be like, however. The rumor is that the show will be directed by rock legend Mark Ravitz, the man behind David Bowie's groundbreaking *Ziggy Stardust* tour. The Millennium Tour kicks off in the States in Miami on September 19, 1999. They plan to perform for three months—and then hurry back home to record a Backstreet Boys Christmas album.

Otherwise, the guys have no huge future plans. Following the tour, they will perhaps start work on their next album, which they are determined will feature at least one song written by each Boy. Also, each Boy wants to get more involved in playing some of the instruments on the album. There were plans for a comic book, illustrated by the group's resident artist, Nick Carter, but it looks like this is moving to the back burner for now. "It's a dark Batman-like story, a sci-fi type of thing, and all the Backstreet Boys are characters. I believe it will open us up to male fans," Nick gushed to *USA Weekend* in January 1999. It will be about "each of us developing a power, like mutants, and battling a group of aliens who are trying to take over the world through music." That will definitely be something to keep an eye out for!

A.J., Nick, Kevin, Brian, and Howie in London, just before they were to return to their homeland.

BACKSTREET QUIZ
How well do you know . . . **The Guys?**

1) Which Boy failed the written part of his driver's test—twice!
a. Nick
b. A.J.
c. Kevin
d. Howie

2) Which of the guys is terrified of flying?
a. Brian
b. Kevin
c. Howie
d. Nick

3) Which of the guys has a second career in real estate?
a. Nick
b. A.J.
c. Howie
d. Brian

4) Who is the only guy with a serious girlfriend?
a. Nick
b. Brian
c. Kevin
d. Howie

5) Which Boy's grandfather was in a barbershop quartet?
a. Kevin
b. A.J.
c. Nick
d. Howie

Answers: 1: b; 2: d; 3: c; 4: b; 5: a

What Are the Guys' Most Embarrassing Moments?

Hey, Backstreet Boy or not, everyone has made his or her share of goof-ups in life. Here are some of the funniest of the guys' embarrassing moments (and believe me—there are lots more where these came from!).

NICK: During a concert, Nick accidentally "pushed" Howie right off the stage and into the audience!

BRIAN: Kicked a shoe off during a dance number. The shoe flew across the stage, and Brian had to keep dancing in his sock until he could make his way over to where the shoe landed!

A.J.: Started a fire during a show in Germany when he accidentally tossed one of his shirts over a light during a costume change!

KEVIN: Slipped on a pack of cigarettes some fan in Europe had thrown up on the stage during a performance as a gift. See how dangerous cigarettes are!

HOWIE: Howie once had to sing his solo completely *a cappella* when the whole sound system went out right in the middle of one of his songs!

The boys say that they are all as close as brothers, and that like brothers, they don't always get along—but they manage to work through their differences and stay together.

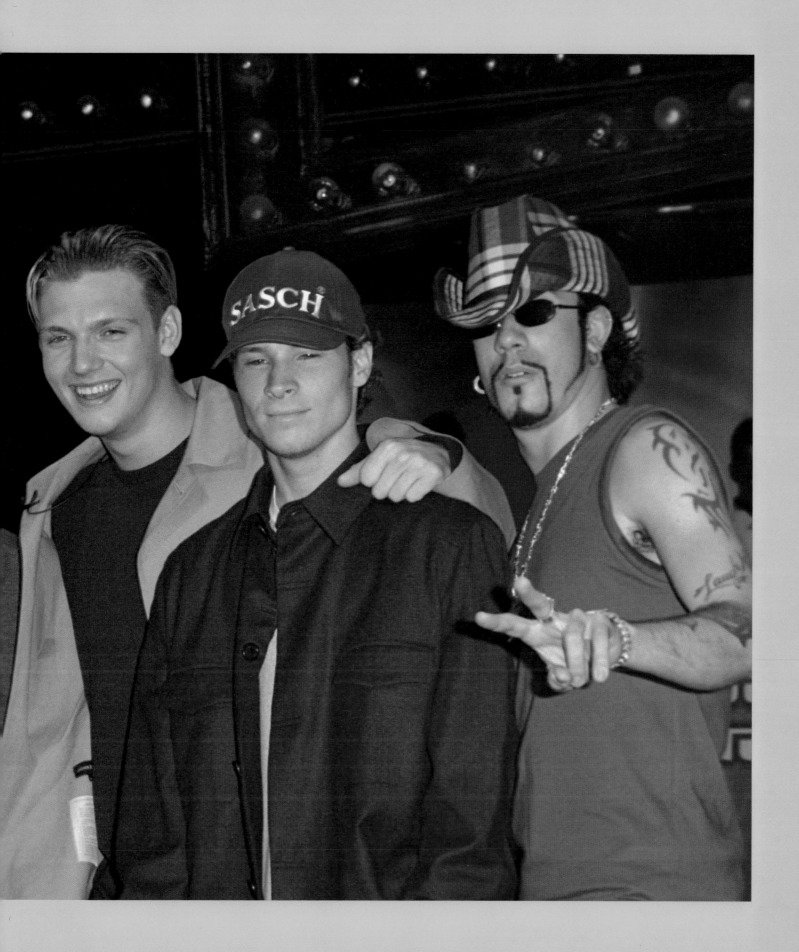

The guys look demure before the 1997 MTV Europe Awards. A year later they would be honored by MTV in the United States.

Bibliography

"Babe Poll Results: The Celebs You Begged For!" *Teen* magazine (September 1998): 84.

"Backstreet Boys Believe: 'You Have to Follow Your Heart.'" *Teen Beat* (August 1999): 70

"Backstreet Boys: Get Ready for the New Millennium." *Teen Beat* (June 1999): 7.

"Backstreet Boys: Interview of the Month." *Teen Beat* (August 1997): 20–21.

"Backstreet's Back with Millennium." *SuperTeen* (August 1999): 26.

Boucher, Geoff. "The Making of Heartthrobs Inc." *Los Angeles Times* (January 24, 1999): 4.

Brooks, Amy and Jeremy Helligar. "Where the Boys Are." *People Weekly* (September 14, 1998): 238.

Brunner, Rob. "Boys Power." *Entertainment Weekly* (June 4, 1999): 9.

Carter, Jane. *The Heart and Soul of Nick Carter*. New York: Penguin Putnam, 1998.

Christman, Ed. "Backstreet Could Hit 1 Mil. In 1st Week." *Billboard* (May 29, 1999): 3.

Cotter, Kelly-Jane. "Backstreet Boys Are the New Heartthrob Act on the Block." Gannett News Service (October 9, 1998)

de Ste. Croix, Philip (editor). *Backstreet Boys: The Unofficial Book*. New York: Billboard Books, 1998.Dunn, Jancee. "The Backstreet Boys' Year in Hell." *Rolling Stone* (May 27, 1999): 42–47.

Farber, Jim. "Where the Boys Are." *Entertainment Weekly* (May 21, 1999): 73.

Finkelstein, Alex. "Backstreet Boy's Firm Sues N.Y. Record Company." Orlando Business Journal (September 18, 1998): 3.

——. "Backstreet Boys: Local Manager Milked Millions." *Orlando Business Journal* (September 11, 1998): 1.

Jaeger, Lauren. "'Everybody' Packing In for Backstreet Boys." *Amusement Business* (July 20, 1998): 1.

Jones, Steve. "Bringing Fame Home: Florida Quintet is Playing 'Games' for Keeps Now." *USA Today* (April 1, 1997): 1D.

Karger, Dave. "Flashes." *Entertainment Weekly* (October 30, 1998): 16.

——. "So Shoot Me!" *Entertainment Weekly* (September 4, 1998): 24.

LeBlanc, Larry. "Backstreet Boys Riding a Wave: Canadian Success Began in Quebec." *Billboard* (December 13, 1997): 52.

"Lunch With Nick and the Backstreet Boys." *SuperTeen* (August 1999): 20–25

Majewski, Lori. "The Boys Are Back." *Teen People* (June/July 1999): 100–04.

Mayfield, Geoff. "Bigger Still." *Billboard* (May 29, 1999): 100.

Nichols, Angie. *Backstreet Boys Confidential: The Unofficial Book*. London: Virgin Books, 1998.

Ross, Mike. "Boys Will Be Boys." *The Edmonton Sun* (May 15, 1999): 44.

Sexton, Paul. "Backstreet Boys Become Global Priority for Jive." *Billboard* (November 1, 1997): 9.

Sinclair, Tom. "The Orlando Magic Backstreet Boys: Florida's Prefab Sprouts Take Root." *Entertainment Weekly* (August 15, 1997): 72.

"The Twenty-one Hottest Stars Under Twenty-one." *Teen People* (June/July 1999): 56.

"25 Most Intriguing People of the Year." *People Weekly* (December 28, 1998): 114.

Weingarten, Marc. "And They Can Sing, Too." *Los Angeles Times* (January 4, 1998).

Zaslow, Jeffrey. "Backstage With the Backstreet Boys." *USA Weekend* (January 10, 1999): 14.

Web Sites

Official International Backstreet Boys Website:
www.backstreetboys.com

Alison's Backstreet Boys Wonderland:
www.geocities.com/SunsetStrip/Backstage/1823

Andrea's Unofficial Backstreet Boys Internet Fan Club:
www.geocities.com/SouthBeach/Lagoon/7620/FrameSet1.html

Anywhere For You:
www.geocities.com/SunsetStrip/Studio/9847/

Backstreet Boys Connection:
www.geocities.com/SunsetStrip/Lounge/3367/

BSB Direct: Backstreet Boys Directory:
surf.to/backstreet.boys/

Jill's Backstreet Boys Heaven:
www.execulink.com/~wmgp/Default.htm

Singapore Backstreet Boys Homepage:
www.ashweb.com/bsb/

T-one's Backstreet Bar:
www.geocities.com/SouthBeach/Surf/4167/

Backstreet Boys Planet:
www.geocities.com/SunsetStrip/Palms/2109/

Backstreet Boys Celebrity Site:
www.bestcelebritysites.com/backstreet-boys

Canadian Backstreet Boys Webring:
www.myna.com/~sacart/ring.htm

Frick and Frack's Backstreet Boys Heaven:
members.tripod.com/~Frick_and_Frack/main.html

Hong Kong Backstreet Boys:
www.geocities.com/SunsetStrip/Lounge/2397/

Yoni's BSB Fantasy:
www.geocities.com/Hollywood/Set/6331

Photography Credits

Index